D0943874

Many roofs are inclined to let snow and rain slide off

Inclined Planes

John Hudson Tiner

A⁺

Smart Apple Media

COPYRIGHT

❏ Published by Smart Apple Media

1980 Lookout Drive, North Mankato, MN 56003

Designed by Rita Marshall

Copyright © 2003 Smart Apple Media. International copyright reserved in all countries. No part of this book may be reproduced in any form without written permission from the publisher.

Printed in the United States of America

❏ Photographs by Gary J. Benson, Richard Cummins, Galyn C. Hammond, The Image Finders (Jim Baron, C. Cassady Jr.), Tom Myers, D. Jeanene Tiner

❏ Library of Congress Cataloging-in-Publication Data

Tiner, John Hudson. Inclined planes / by John Tiner. p. cm. – (Simple machines)

Includes bibliographical references.

Summary: Discusses inclined planes and the ways in which they are used.

❏ ISBN 1-58340-138-5

1. Simple machines–Juvenile literature. 2. Inclined planes–Juvenile literature.

[1. Inclined planes.] I. Title.

TJ147 .T487 2002   621.8'11–dc21   2001054163

❏ First Edition 9 8 7 6 5 4 3 2 1

Inclined Planes

CONTENTS

Making Travel Easier

The Grand **Canyon** is a deep valley in the western United States. Trails out of it switch back and forth to follow a gentle slope. Hiking the trails is easier than climbing straight up the steep canyon walls. Each trail is an example of an **inclined plane**. The word "inclined" means sloped. A plane is a flat surface. ☐ An inclined plane can work without moving. Instead, objects move along it. A road over a mountain may be built like an inclined plane. The mountain may be cut down, and valleys may be filled in. The slope is made more gradual,

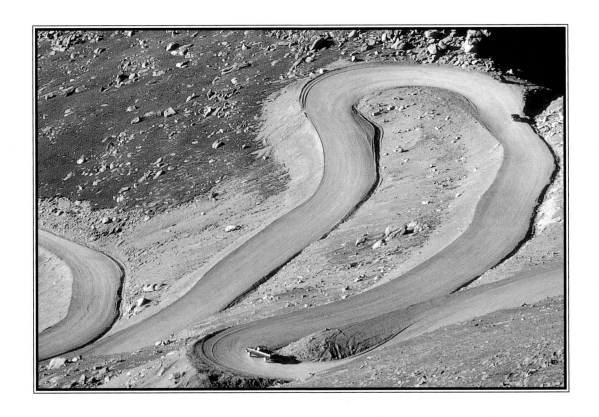

making it easier for trucks to pull heavy trailers over the

mountain. ☐ Many trucks carry a loading ramp. A loading

ramp is an inclined plane. Workers roll objects along the ramp

Inclined planes can make a mountain slope less steep

and into the truck. It is easier than lifting the weight straight

up. But distance is traded for the reduced effort. In other

words, the load seems lighter but it has to be pushed farther.

Pushing Things Apart

A wedge is a tool with two inclined planes put back

to back. Wedges are used to push things apart. Today, wedges

can be found everywhere. An axe is a type of wedge. Pencil

sharpeners have wedge-like blades. Knives and the cutting

edges of can openers are wedges. So are the points of needles

and the ends of nails. ☐ A person has to look closely at a nail

to tell that it is a wedge. The point of a nail is sharpened so

that it has two to four sloping surfaces. Each of the surfaces is

an inclined plane. Hammering a nail into a block of wood

Nails' wedge points make them easier to hammer in

Hikers walk out of the Grand Canyon on inclined trails

would be difficult if the end were blunt. Because of its wedge shape, a nail makes a hole in the wood that starts small and gets bigger.

Holding Things Together

A ramp can be made more compact by wrapping it around and around. Some playgrounds have spiral-shaped slides. A spiral staircase is another example of this space-saving shape. Towers in the ancient city of Babylon had spiral ramps around them. People walked to the top by going around and

Some forms of inclined planes are fun, such as spiral slides

around. ☐ A screw is an inclined plane wrapped around a cylinder. From one end of a screw to the other is one long ramp, like a spiral staircase. But unlike a ramp, a screw does move. It has to be turned. ☐ Screws that hold boards together are called wood screws. The ends are sharpened so they cut into the wood. A person

Many public buildings have ramps for people in wheelchairs. Ramps make it much easier to roll wheelchairs into buildings.

turns the screws with a screwdriver. Screws that hold metal parts together are called machine screws. A machine screw comes in two parts. One part is the bolt, and the other

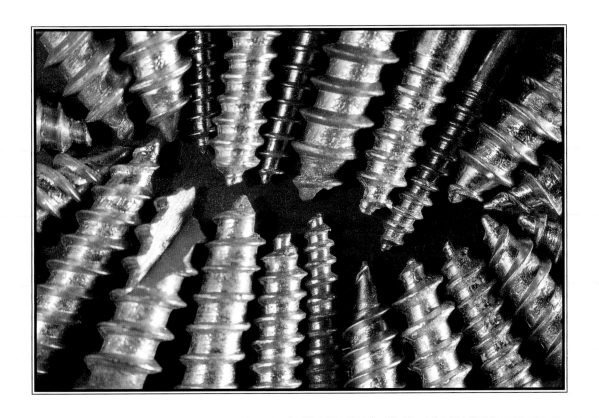

part is the nut. The bolt is slipped through a hole in each piece of metal. Tightening the nut on the bolt holds the metal parts together.

Screws have inclined planes wrapped around them

South Main School
Learning Resource Center

Presses and Jacks

The first screws were large and were turned with wooden handles. As the screws were turned, they passed through a nut and pressed a flat board against another board. Grapes were put between the boards. Screw presses squeezed juice from the grapes. ▢ The

An airplane propeller is a type of screw. By turning rapidly, the propeller helps pull the airplane through the air.

first **printing press** was a screw press. Turning a handle pressed a sheet of paper against metal bars called type. The

This screw press was used to squeeze oil from olives

16

bars of type had letters on one side coated with ink. The sheet of paper was pressed against the letters, and ink came off on the paper. The first books were printed this way. ☐ A jack is a large screw made to raise heavy objects. One common use for a jack is to lift a car so a flat tire can be changed. Some giant jacks are so powerful that they can lift the corner of a building. To lift the building, the jack must be turned many times. ☐ Inclined planes, ramps,

Screw-on lids and the jars on which they fit are examples of two screws that fit together like a bolt and nut.

Jacks are large screws that can be used to lift a car

and screws can be found throughout a person's home. A drill bit for boring holes is a type of inclined plane. So is the clamp of a vise. Many foods and beverages are stored in jars or bottles with screw-on lids or caps. Under some washers and dryers are leveling screws. Turning these screws makes the appliance sit level. In these and many other forms, inclined planes help us every day.

A farmer's plow is a type of inclined plane. It breaks up the ground so that seeds can be planted.

A screw-on jar lid is a commonly used inclined plane

An Inclined Plane Experiment

This experiment will prove that it is easier to roll a load up a long, sloped ramp than up a short, steep one.

What You Need

A toy truck

Two boards, one longer than the other

A rubber band

A stack of books about six inches (15 cm) high

Strong string about two feet (61 cm) long

What You Do

1. Tie the string to the rubber band.
2. Tie the other end of the string to the front of the truck.
3. Make a ramp with the shorter board by placing one end on the stack of books.
4. Hold the rubber band and slowly pull the truck up the ramp. Watch how much the rubber band stretches.
5. Repeat steps 3 and 4 with the longer ramp.

What You See

The stretch in the rubber band shows how hard it is to pull the truck along the ramp. The truck is easier to pull up the longer ramp, but it has to be pulled farther.

Driving up a hill is easier if the road is long and sloped

Index

Words to Know

appliance (uh-PLY-unss)—a device, usually one that runs on electricity, that does a specific job

canyon (CAN-yun)—a narrow valley with steep walls usually cut by a river

inclined plane (in-KLINED PLANE)—a flat surface set at an angle; an inclined plane is a simple machine

printing press (PRINT-ing press)—a machine that transfers lettering to paper by pressing the paper against an inked surface

propeller (pruh-PEH-ler)—rotating blades that move a ship through water or an airplane through air

Read More

Ardley, Neil. *The Science Book of Machines*. London: Dorling Kindersley Limited, 1992.

Hodge, Deborah. *Simple Machines*. Buffalo, N.Y.: Kids Can Press, 1998.

Taylor, Barbara. *Force and Movement*. New York: Franklin Watts, 1990.

Internet Sites

Brain Pop™ Health and Science
http://www.brainpop.com/tech/simple machines/inclinedplane/index.weml

MIKIDS.COM: Inclined Planes
http://www.mikids.com/SMachines InclinedPlanes.htm

Simple Machines Learning Site
http://www.coe.uh.edu/archive/science/sciencelessons/scienceles1/finalhome.htm